Foreword

I have long been amazed at the "Mayo-God-help us" attitude of people who [illegible] know better and I have been surprised by the ignorance of many on this little island (3 hours x 5 hours) who have never visited the counties of Ireland. So many Mayo people have 'stood up and been counted'. So many have risen to the top in their various professions, that we are indeed proud.

I hope that this little book will surely show that God has indeed helped us.

Pat Walsh,
Claremorris.

Acknowledgements

My thanks to the following for permission to reproduce photographs:

Irish Times:	Mary Robinson
G.A.A.:	P.W. Nally
Anne Chambers, Murrisk:	Margaret Sheridan
Ann Ward, Claremorris:	Delia Murphy
Fr. Fintan Monaghan	Archbishop McHale
Bishop's House, Tuam	Other Bishops
Maureen Walsh, Kiltimagh:	Louis Walsh
Fine Gael & Labour Parties	Party Leaders
Jarlath Cunnane, Castlebar	Northabout
Cormac Hanley, Claremorris	Cameron Hanley
Dr. Roderick Maguire	Conor Maguire
An Garda Siochána	Commissioner Conroy
Davitt Museum	Michael Davitt

Old Head Pier Louisburgh

Children, adults and boatmen enjoy a day at the sea, on this Blue Flag beach.

Old Head With Blue Flag

Relax and build
a few sand castles…!

Old Head front view

You can have an ice cream too between swims.

Old Head right view

Relax and chill out here

Atlantic Drive – Achill Island

Beauty that speaks for itself

Rocks v Atlantic

Where the immovable object meets the irresistible force!

Atlantic Drive – Achill Island

A beautiful
Atlantic Drive

Outside Newport

Get an eye-full of this...

Newport Hills

Ah! Beautiful to see!
Let's go for a stroll.

Mulranny

Take a day off and chill out!

Croagh Patrick

Is it playing "hide and seek"?
Let's go climb it.

Croagh Patrick (The Reek) Across Wooded Hills

Mayo's Holy Mountain: a 760m high pyramid (East view) and place of annual prayer pilgrimage climbed by many on last Sunday in July each year. Great views of Clew Bay and Islands.

Westport Under The Reek

A planned and beautiful town,
Westport nestles under Croagh Patrick.

Here you will find many excellent
restaurants, hotels, pubs, shops,
sea fishing, sailing, golf and 'the craic'.

Westport Bridge and Fountain

Westport is
a winner of the national
"Irish Tidy Towns Competition"

Westport Boats

A lively sailing Club.
There is another (Glenans) nearby.

Coislough

For peace, tranquillity and good trout fishing at Ballinrobe.

When enough fishing is done you could 'slip out to the Horse Races'.

At the Mayo-Galway Border, Cong

Come boating, fishing, or for a picnic!

Grazing on the Mayo-Galway Border

Happy cows! Happy people!

Mary Robinson

Ballina

Ex President of Ireland,
then U.N. High Commissioner
for Human Rights, 1997 to 2002.

Commissioner Noel Conroy

Blacksod

Retired head of the Irish Police
(An Garda Siochána)

Fr. Enda McDonagh
Bekan & Maynooth

Professor of Moral Theology, Saint Patrick's College, Maynooth University. Priest and Esteemed Writer.

Monsignor James Horan
Born Tourmakeady 1911. P.P. Tooreen and Knock

Priest, Leader, Multi-project Manager. Responsible for building a famous dance hall in Tooreen. This was an important social venue in the 50's and 60's. He re-defined Knock village and built the Basilica and parks around it. Monsignor Horan was responsible for the planning and development of Ireland West Airport Knock which is a huge contributor to Mayo's march to prosperity. He also instigated building roads and planting forests.
Was the chief advocate in bringing Pope John Paul II to Knock.

Enda Kenny
T.D.
Castlebar

Leader of the second largest party
(Fine Gael) in Dáil Eireann
(the Irish Parliament)

Pat Rabbitte
T.D.
Ballindine

Leader of the third largest party
(Labour) in Dáil Eireann
until April 2007.

Padraig Flynn
N.T., T.D.
Castlebar

Government Minister and European Commissioner (Fianna Fail). Padraig entered politics in the 60s, was elected to Mayo C.C. in 1967, to Dail Eireann in 1977. He became Minister for the Environment, for Justice and for Industry & Commmerce in the years 1980 to 1993. He was European Commissioner for Employment & Social Affairs from 1993 to 1999.

Admiral William Brown

Foxford (1977–1857)

Founder of the Argentine Navy. Much revered in Argentina where more than 1200 streets are named after him.

Michael Davitt

Straide (1849–1906)

Born in Famine years, evicted from home, with parents and siblings, at age 4. Emigrated to England, worked in cotton mills, lost an arm, got involved in social work with Irish community there. Patriot, World traveller, Politician, Fenian.

Founded the "Land League" in 1879. This was of extreme importance to all Irish small farmers. Worked with Parnell.

Sean Lavan

Kiltimagh (1898-1973)

Teacher, Surgeon, Gaelic Footballer, Rugby Player, Hurler & Handballer. 1920 became All-Ireland Handball Champion. 1921 was on Mayo team against Dublin (Semi-Final) when he introduced the solo-run to Gaelic football. 1923 Member UCD Sigerson winning team in Belfast. Established many Athletics records. 1924 & 1928 took part in Olympics in Paris & Amsterdam.

P.W. Nally

Balla (1857–1891)

Athlete, Footballer, Fenian. In 1879 he organised the first National Athletic Sports on his fathers lands in Balla to start wresting sports control from the Landlords and promote Gaelic games. Worked closely with the like-minded Ml. Cusack and was a member of the GAA founder group in 1884. Died mysteriously in jail for Ireland's cause the week before due for release, in same year as Parnell. The Nally Stand in Croke Park was erected in his honour (as was the Cusack stand for Ml. Cusack.)

Martin Sheridan

Bohola (1881–1918)

One of the greatest Olympians of the 20th century (for his adopted country USA) won 5 Gold, 3 Silver 1 Bronze in discuss-throwing, high jump, shot-putt and pole vault.

Cameron Hanley
Claremorris

Of the Claremorris School of Equitation. Won the Kerry Gold Grand Prix in the RDS in 2000.
Won King George V Gold Cup at Hickstead in 2000. A member of the Irish Team Aga Khan Cup in 2007.
Had recent success in a World Ranking Competition in Oldenburg, Germany.

Niamh Kitching
Claremorris

Golfer & teacher. Winner of Ladies Scratch Cup (Ireland) 2006.
Member Irish Universities team. Won Silver in Thailand at World University Championships. Captain University of Limerick Intervarsity Team.
In 2007 the R & A picked her with an Icelander for the Argentinean Open.
On the Irish Ladies Home International team.

Margaret Burke Sheridan

Castlebar

(1889–1958)

Opera Singer. Ireland's first Prima Donna. Soprano, sang at Covent Garden, La Scala (Milan), Rome and San Carlo (Naples). Dearly loved by the Italians for her 'golden' voice and warm personality: a great interpreter of Puccini and Toscanini. Made many recordings for HMV (Red labels).

Delia Murphy B.Comm

Mount Jennings Hollymount

(1902–1971)

Singer, Collector and Recorder of hundreds of Irish ballads.
Married to Irish diplomat Tom Kiernan.
Lived and sang in many countries for 'The Irish'. Recorded 72 songs, 45 of them for HMV.

Bill O'Dwyer

Bohola

(1890–1964)

Graduated Fordham University 1923.
Brigadier General U.S. army.
Mayor of New York 1945-1950.
Ambassador to Mexico 1952

Louis Walsh

Kiltimagh

TV personality ("You're a Star" "The X Factor").
Businessman and top of the game in Pop-Band Management.
Discoverer of pop talent and manager of "Boyzone" and "Westlife" bands as well as Ronan Keating, Lulu, Samantha Mumba and others.

Emily McManus

Kiltimagh

Author.
Matron of Guys Hospital, London during WW 2 and the London Blitz.

Michael Hogarty

Kiltimagh

Born 1918 (approx.)

Emigrated with parents to USA in 1930. Engineer. Very involved with US Army in WW2. Member of elite engineers who made B29 bomber having computerised the bombsiting of that aircraft. Was on many missions over Japan including the last. Awarded the 'Flying Cross' and the 'Air Medal' with 4 Oaks Leaf Cluster and a Presidential Citation.

Louis Brennan

Castlebar

(1852–1932)

Invented the first guided torpedo. Worked on early helicopter design and gyroscope balancers for monorail trains.
Emigrated to Australia where he got Government aid for his work.

Grace O'Malley

Clare Island

(1530–1603)

"The Pirate Queen". A brave and daring lady with excellent sailing skills. She had well honed and much practiced diplomatic skills too: skills that enabled her to secure a visit and private audience with Queen Elizabeth in London at a time of constant war between Ireland and England. Ireland at this time was divided into many small Kingdoms approximately two or three counties in size. Hers was a "queendom" around Clew Bay, Clare Island, North Galway and Mayo where she built many castles. She ran her own "customs and excise" in the area and was an excellent merchant trader. She had three sons.

Conor Maguire

Cong

(1889–1971)

1914 Solicitors practice Claremorris,
1932 T.D. and Attorney General,
1936 High Court Judge,
1946 Chief Justice.

Cardinal John D'Alton

Claremorris

(1882–1963)

Renowned scholar and R.C. Clergyman. Became Bishop of Meath then Archbishop of Armagh and in Nov. 1952 he was made Cardinal and Primate of All Ireland by Pope Pius XII.
He was a distinguished scholar with many degrees and Doctorates.

Archbishop John McHale

Tubbernavine, Castlebar. (1791–1881)

Educated in Castlebar and Maynooth. Was Archbishop of the (very large) diocese of Tuam during the Famine years. Did a lot of work to relieve famine stress. Was very involved in the politics of the day. Had many a scuffle with British officials and also other Irish Bishops regarding education.

Three Archbishops

Tuam Diocese

Former Archbishops of Tuam
Dr. Michael Neary, Dr. Joseph Cunnane
and Dr. Joseph Cassidy,
– all Mayo men.

Jarlath Cunnane

Knock. (Born 1938)

Skipper of 'NORTHABOUT' a boat which he built himself making it strong enough to sail the 'North East Passage' over the "top of the World" and North of the Arctic Circle through ice fields and danger. The project started in 2001 and finished in Westport in 2005. It covered 7500 miles, 3000 of this being ice and with 3 ice "bottlenecks". The challenge was to be the first small yacht to go Pacific to Atlantic as the time-frame is only 2 months. Two of the crew now work in Mayo, they are Dr Michael Brogan in Ballyhaunis and Rory Casey (Fibre Optics) in Castlebar. The rest of the crew: Paddy Barry, Garry Finnegan, Colm Brogan, Kevin Cronin, Vladislow Samoilovich (ice navigator) and on shore keeping radio contact was Brendan Minish. Jarlath also lives in Mayo. (Website: www.northabout.com)

Pictured above right: Jarlath Cunnane.

Centre left: crew of Northabout.

Right: Dr. Michael Brogan.

Below: Northabout in ice.

Emigrant Ship Murrisk

Start of The Reek climb. A replica to remind all of the massive emigration from Mayo during The Great Famine of 1846- '47.
Emigration was high for over another century.

Museum of Country Life, Turlough

Set in beautiful grounds and near the Round Tower this museum, like all museums, tells us a lot of history about rural life 'way back'.

Ashford Castle, Cong

Five Star Hotel. Restful resort for rich and famous from all over the world. It has its own Golf course, boat jetty, excellent fishing, a Falconry and beautiful garden walks.

Claremorris Golf Club

One of ten Golf Courses in Mayo.

Swimming Pool

One of twenty such pools in the county.

McWilliam Park Hotel, Claremorris

Ballina Fishing – Ridgepool

Recognised as one of the best salmon fishing rivers in Europe.

Turlough Round Tower

Turlough, Castlebar

A fine, well preserved example of round towers. These towers were built as places of refuge from enemy raiding parties in the 9th to 12th century. It was in the ownership of the Bourks and later the Fitzgerald families around 1655.

Ballinsmalla Carmelite Monastery

Claremorris

Established in 1288. Declined to near oblivion and was re-opened in 1702 under a Fr Peter Hughes; becoming a centre for the rebirth if the Irish Carmelite Province. Here youth were received, given an early education and then sent on to France or Spain for "second and third level" for ordination to the priesthood. It was, as any monastery, a place of prayer and the contemplative life and a burial ground. Carmelite priests here did much work with the poor and the sick as well as educating. It was in "full swing" in 1730 but by 1823 it was one of only 9 Carmelite monasteries in Ireland. It closed in 1870 25 years after the great famine which caused massive death and emigration.

Shrine Grounds & Basilica, Knock

A very popular Marion Shrine where thousands of pilgrims come to pray each year.

Interior of Basilica

Ballintubber Abbey (near Castlebar)

Founded in 1216. Mass has been celebrated here continuously despite attack and religious persecution. King Cathal O'Connor was the founder and it is the only church founded by an Irish King that is still in use.

This is a very popular venue for weddings.

Ballintubber Abbey Sanctuary and Aisle

Knock Airport

Ireland West Airport Knock. Started very small in 1985, now has flights to 23 destinations in Europe with more coming on stream.

McHale Park Castlebar

Mayo has fifty GAA clubs. Ladies as well as men are prominent in these sports in the county. The Senior mens team were in the All-Ireland Final in 2006. The Mayo senior ladies won their All-Ireland in 1999, 2000,2002 and 2003. There are many excellent GAA grounds with full facilities around the county: pictured is McHale Park in Castlebar.

GMIT, Castlebar

Galway-Mayo Institute of Technology: a Third Level College educating Mayo into the technological era.

Mid-West Radio (MWRfm) Ballyhaunis

One of the most successful local radio stations in Ireland.

N17 Road & Bridge

No donkeys here!

Castlebar Industrial Park

Started in 1985.
It is growing at a
fast rate since.

Communication Tower Castlebar

Reaching out to Business,
Emigrants, Tourists and Friends.
One of several in the county.

Mayo Construction

A typical sight
nowadays.

Typical modern landscapes of the Mayo built environment: not an (endearing?) thatched cottage to be seen!

The New Mayo Built Landscape

Wind Turbines

There are 28 of these in Mayo producing electricity for the National Grid. Many more are planned.

Mayo Broadband

Part of the new 'Super Highways ' of Mayo

McHale Agricultural Machinery Factory, Ballinrobe

At their factory in Ballinrobe McHales design, develop and build Agricultural machines of many types. They are exported to 56 countries worldwide.

Foxford Woollen Mills

Foxford Woollen Mills, suppliers of beautiful tweeds, blankets, scarves etc. to Europe, the U.S. and Japan is very proud of its products. Visitors are welcome.

The Mill was founded in 1892 by Sr Morrough Bernard of the Irish Sisters of Charity to help relieve poverty in the area. By 1948 there were 250 workers employed here as people all over the World knew and respected the 'Foxford' label on woollen goods.

With the arrival of synthetic fibres and the duvet demand declined and the Mill went into receivership in 1987 but it never closed. It was bought by the present owners and to this day it is a 'working mill' producing top class woollen products. (Visit and see). It now has two shops in Dublin, one in Westport and one in Moygashel Dungannon as people discovered again the superior quality and value of woollen products. The traditional blanket is still made there among many other new and beautiful designs.

FOXFORD

FOXFORD
WOOLLEN MILLS
EST. 1892

FOXFORD

FOXFORD

MOONLIGHT IN MAYO

It's just a year ago to-day I left dear Erin's Isle
My heart was throbbing in the sun light of my girlfriend's smile
In all my dreams I seem to hear her sweet voice soft and low
I know she's waiting where we said good bye in old Mayo.

CHORUS:

For two Irish eyes are smiling and an Irish heart is pining
Where I kissed her and caressed her in the gloaming long ago
Loving Irish arms will press me and sweet Irish lips caress me
And true Irish love will bless me when it's Moonlight in Mayo

Her Irish eyes like beacons shine all through the darkest night
I know their soft love-beams will always fill the world with light
The roses on her cheeks will lend enchantment to the scene
And when the shamrock wears the dew I'll wed my sweet colleen.

CHORUS

The following song is a parody on 'Moonlight in Mayo' (opposite) and it gives a good insight into daily life conditions in Mayo during WWII when rationing of goods was imposed by the Government and was enforced (sometimes!!) by the police. Like poteen making some illicit practices went on, such as sifting the crude brown flour to get white flour by "using a piece of silk". Petrol, cigarettes and other imports were extremely scarce. Oil lamps were still in use in many rural areas at this time.

It's just a year ago to-day they blacked out Erin's Isle
And left us in the darkness when they rationed light and oil
In all the shops we see the cops they're searching high and low
We know they're looking for the names on forms to K.O.
Now the Irish sight is failing and the good days were bewailing
When we trimmed our lamps at twilight in the gloaming long ago
As in darkness we're undressing the officials we're not blessing
Soon there'll be no light were guessing
But the Moonlight in Mayo.

The cigarettes are hard to get, were searching till were sick
They always say "we've none to-day we'll have them in next week"
While Churchill smokes a fat cigar and talks of 'lend & lease'
The boys at home would much prefer to smoke the pipe of peace
Now the white roots we are smoking make us cough until were choking
In our pockets we are hoking for the butts we used to throw
But we'll have to wait in patience 'till the train comes to the station
Then we'll shout with wild elation "There's Woodbines in Mayo".

The flour that should be white is brown, far browner than the turf
The tea that should be brown is white; you'll say that's fair enough
When we had neither tea nor flower we lived on spuds and milk.
No brown flour now, for we know how to use the piece of silk
Now on white bread we are living and no information giving
As to how they do their sieving or where they get the dough
T'is a secret how they make it but they sift it and they shake it
And were told they only bake it when its Moonlight in Mayo.

MAYO

Killala Bay
Lough Conn
Achill Island
Clew Bay
Castlebar
N5
Claremorris
Lough Mask
N17
Connemara
Lough Corrib